TIME SPACE AND DRUMS SUPPLEMENTAL

COMMON DRUMMING QUESTIONS

Frequently Asked Questions for Drummers Just Starting Out

TIME SPACE AND DRUMS SUPPLEMENTAL

COMMON DRUMMING QUESTIONS

Frequently Asked Questions for Drummers Just Starting Out

The Time Space & Drums Series
A Complete Program of Lessons in Professional, Contemporary Rock, and Jazz Drumming Styles.

Written and Developed By:
Stephen Hawkins

Graphic Design By: Nathaniel Dasco.
Special Thanks To Linda Drouin and Ikhide Oshoma

ThinkeLife Publications

Time Space and Drums Copyright 2020 By Stephen Hawkins.

All Rights Reserved.

No part of this book may be reproduced in any form or by any electronic or mechanical means including information storage and retrieval means without permission in writing from the author.

The only exception is by a reviewer, who may quote short excerpts in a review.

Stephen Hawkins - Time Space and Drums
Visit my website at www.timespaceanddrums.com

First printing: Aug 2020.

ISBN: 978 1 913929 26 8

Dedicated to the late Paul Daniels and family, Martin Daniels, Trevor Daniels, Paul Mellor's, Keith, Peter Windle, Andrew Marple's, Colin Keys, Peters & Lee, Susan Maughan, Ronnie Dukes, Tom O'Connor, Les Dennis, Bob Monkhouse, Bobby Davro, Tommy Bruce, Robert Young, Sandie Gold as well as the hundreds of other people who have played a part in my life experience. Including Sphinx Entertainment, E & B Productions as well as the hundreds of fantastic personalities I have had the pleasure of working alongside over the past 35 years. Apologies for anyone I have missed, not forgetting the current reader who I hope will receive as much from their drumming as I have and more – Stephen Hawkins.

Table of Contents

INTRODUCTION 1

Question: What Are Some Good Drumming Songs? 1

Question: What Do the Numbers on Drum Sticks Mean? 3

Question: Does Drumming Help Improve Muscle Strength? 4

Question: How Do I Get a Drumming Sponsorship from a Drum Company? 5

Question: Beatles Songs That Have the Best of Ringo's Drumming? 6

Question: How Can I Get Motivated as A Drummer? 7

Question: Are Electronic Drum Kits OK for a Beginner to Learn On? 9

Question: I Have Good Speed with My Right but My Left Lacking in Speed. ... 10

Question: How Should I Expand A Drum Kit? 12

Question: Can You Recommend a Beginner Drummer DVD? 15

Question: What Does It Really Take to Be A Drummer in A Band? 16

Question: I Want to Play the Drums for Someone Famous – How Do I Do It?. 17

Question: Who Are the Best Drummers in Rock? 17

Question: How Should I Store My Drums? 18

Question: What Do I Need to Play My Electronic Drum Kit Live? 19

Question: Should I polish my cymbals? 20

Question: How Do I Stop My Bass Drum and Hi-hat Pedals Creeping? 21

Question: Why Should I Cut A Hole in My Bass Drum Head? 22

Question: Can I Fix My Broken Cymbals? 23

Question: How Should I Tune My Resonant Heads? 24

Question: What's the Best Way to Tame Snare Drum Buzz? 26

Question: What's the Secret to A Low, Booming Bass Drum Sound? 27

Question: What's the Difference Between Steel and Synthetic Drum Shells?. 28

Question: Can I Learn to Play the Drums Without a Drum Kit? 30

Question: When Should A Drummer Who Is Just Starting Get a Drum Kit? 30

Question: Where's the Best Place to Buy Drums? 31

Question: How High Should I Setup My Snare Drum, Tom, and Cymbals? 32

Question: I'm Left Handed - Do I Set My Drums Up Differently? 32
Question: Can I Teach Myself to Play the Drums or Do I Need A Teacher? 33
Question: How Do I Find & Choose A Drum Teacher? 34
Question: How Often Should I Be Practising the Drums? 36
Question: What Should I Practice? 38
Question: Do I Need to Read Music to Play the Drums? 39
Question: So Why Do People Learn to Read Music? 39
Question: Is Learning to Read Music Hard? 40
Question: How Can I Make My Drums Quieter? 40
Question: Can You Learn to Play Drums on An Electronic Kit? 41
Question: Would You Recommend Electronic Drums? 42
Question: Do I Have to Live in A Specific Area to Start the Course? 42
Question: Can You Explain the Price of The Course, It Seems Expensive? 42
Question: Do You Offer Private One-On-One Drum Lessons? 42
Question: Do I Need to Have A Drum Teacher as Well? 43
Question: Are There Updates Available? 43
Question: What Do I Get If I Start on The Course? 43
Question: Why Doesn't the Course Include Videos? 43
Question: Can the Program Really Make Me a Great Drummer? 44
Question: Can You Explain the Time Space & Drums Formula Some More? 44
Question: Why Do You Speak of The Universe? 44
Question: I Don't Have A Great Deal of Time, Will That Be A Problem? 45
Question: What If There Is Something I Don't Understand on The Course? 45
Question: Do I Have to Take the Whole Course? 45
Question: What Do I Need to Get Started on The Program? 45
Question: How Do I Start on The Program? 46
Question: What Makes This Course So Different? 46

INTRODUCTION

Many drummers just starting out have approached me with many questions over the years and especially since I produced and published the Time Space & Drums Series of books.

What follows then are the most common questions along with some answers that I put together from a variety of sources plus an end comment that I think should be a guiding note regarding the subject matter.

Here goes:

Question: What Are Some Good Drumming Songs?
Please include songs that have insanely awesome drum parts.

TSD ANSWER: It completely depends on your ability. Music is the same as drumming... It's not worth looking at step 10 if you haven't completed step 1 yet. The songs you should concentrate on should be songs that center around the level of drumming that you are learning at the time.

Having said that, for inspiration and to add focus to your current playing abilities as well as giving you a more rounded drumming foundation to build on I recommend listening to the drummers that follow.

But first, as a drummer learning odd timing can help advance your drumming foundation (see part 5) and so I highly recommend Bill Bruford. He played with a band called U.K. in their earlier recordings and also played in his own band called Bruford as well as some early Genesis and other recordings.

He plays some amazingly complex rhythms yet in a simple way. They do say that "it's not what you do it's the way that you do it," so I highly recommend anything of Bills.

In particular the Bruford albums:

Feels Good to Me
Bruford
One of a Kind

He has always served as a foundation for more complex drumming from my own perspective.
Stephen Hawkins

Moving on from Bill Bruford, Terry Bozzio is a good place to hear some great drumming. In fact, anything that Frank Zappa recorded with Terry Bozzio on drums is usually outstanding.

The closest I ever got to listening to pop music was the band called The Police. All of their albums contain some great straight-ahead drumming usually with a reggae Latin kind of a feel to it. But great with it. Especially the album "Regatta De Blank".

In the contemporary arena, you can't beat my all-time favorite Dave Weckl. In particular, the original version of "Island Magic" was recorded on his "The Next Step Video".

Dave continues to astound many drummers and no doubt will continue for many years to come. I believe Dave Weckl and Chick Corea and the rest of those musicians that stem from The Chick Corea Electric Band changed the face of contemporary music today. They took it to a whole new level. But that's my personal view. Got a Match from the first Electric Band album is an absolute must-listen.

My next recommendation should go without saying. Buddy Rich. Anything he ever recorded contains s-ma astounding drumming and for me especially the albums:

The Man from Planet Jazz – recorded live at Ronnie Scots.

But a good starting point is the Album titled: The Buddy Rich Collection – Buddy Rich Big Band.

But seriously anything that contains Buddy Rich.

As a side note, a great contemporary rock band well worth a listen is Gino Vannelli, in particular, the Brother-to-Brother Album.

I could go on forever but without knowing a particular drummer's ability it is difficult to suggest any worthwhile listening but in general anything with the following drummers and musicians are worth a listen.

Buddy Rich, Dave Weckl, David Garibaldi (Tower of Power), The Brecker Brothers, Chuck Mangione (especially Live at The Hollywood Bowl with James Bradley Junior on drums), Chad Wackerman, Frank Zappa, Bill Bruford, Terry Bozzio, Vinny Colaiuta, Michel Camilo, Dave Grusin, Lee Ritenour.

These are my favorite musicians and bands and of course, I have many more but these are really the top bands and musicians for me. I much prefer the American contemporary and jazz style music and the variations of those styles.

When I was starting out if I discovered a song or particular piece of drumming that I liked I went to a local second-hand record store and searched through every album looking for the drummers I would discover. Also, I would visit the local town to find albums containing drumming by the one who influenced me.

It is all really down to personal choice and so I can only hope that I have touched on something here in regards to the original question which I did try to keep in mind as I wrote this.

Question: What Do the Numbers on Drum Sticks Mean?

Which number is best for side drumming?

TSD ANSWER: The number that is embedded into the drum stick relates to the thickness of the stick. The lower the number is, the thicker the stick gets. If you have large hands you may want to choose something like a 2A or 2B stick.

More contemporary and jazz drummers use a thinner stick, something like 7a.

In the beginning and periodically as you develop it's a good idea to try out different sticks to find the most comfortable ones for you.

Depending on the style of music you play you may need to choose thicker sticks but bear in mind the end result. I.e., You will most likely be miked up through a large P.A System. If that is the case you may want to concentrate more on the finesse a stick helps you produce rather than choosing a stick purely based on maximizing your volume.

Jazz drummers use the thinner sticks for the additional finesse that is produced with cymbals and hi-hats. If you're purely a Rock Drummer you could make a switch between a "standard" 5B stick and a 7A.

The letter after the number describes the shoulder or taper of the stick at the tip. You could say it describes the feel of them.

You should spend time trying and playing with different sizes to see what works best for you regarding the feel of the stick but knowing the music you will be playing and the environmental factors. Try 2's, 5's, and 7's.

You can make a quick choice based on your hand size but if after 15 minutes of playing with those sticks your hands get tired or you start getting blisters then there is most likely something wrong with your stick choice.

You should also pay attention to the stick tip. Wooden tips are more durable than the nylon tips but the nylon tips are much louder. They always seem too harsh for me personally. Wooden tips produce a warmer sound and volume isn't necessarily what I look for.

Question: Does Drumming Help Improve Muscle Strength?
If I practice an hour a day will that improve muscle?

TSD ANSWER: In my early years I believed drumming was all about physical activity and the use of muscle. To that end, I believe it did keep me toned but that was more to do with the constant drumming rather than drumming in and of itself.

Although I was weight training at the time, I do believe that my drumming kept me slim, simply because it wasn't a case of an hour at the gym every day then resting the muscles. It was more like an hour at the gym every day if I could be bothered because I was drumming all day?

In the end, drumming isn't about building muscle. It's about playing music.

Instead, drumming is about using the muscle you do have to perform with more ease, less sweat, and producing a better sound.

The endorphins created whilst exercising may possibly increase when drumming but it is my uneducated assumption that they do not increase. But that may be because as I said, drumming is about using the muscle you already have rather than creating bigger muscles.

At best I believe the long hours of drumming may help keep your metabolism high, therefore you burn more fat and so you may appear slimmer and more defined in the muscle area. But I have also seen some large chaps play drums like nobody's business.

From my own perspective, the most important added benefit of drumming is more to do with the immune and lymphatic system.

The blood or circulatory system has the heart to pump the blood around the body. But lymph fluid does not have a pump. Lymph fluid comes from the blood through a capillary bed into the lymphatic system where it moves into lymph nodes and eliminates toxins through the various glands.

When the lymph fluid leaves the capillaries and enters the Lymphatic System, the lymph fluid needs a way to eliminate the toxins by a constant flow or motion which can only be produced by physical movement and I believe some massage techniques which again is essentially movement.

So, movement helps you move the toxins from the body which makes the immune system stronger.

That to me is a much better benefit to the body than gaining muscle through drumming.

Question: How Do I Get a Drumming Sponsorship from a Drum Company?

Companies like Pearl, Premier, Paiste, Zildjian, and Sabian for instance.

TSD ANSWER: Okay, let's look at some of the practical steps including:
Find the drum companies address and send the drum companies Artist Relations Department a CD, DVD, or Demo Packages of your playing.

Many drum companies also have a website with a specific for you need to fill in if you are looking for an endorsement.

However, those practical steps may not be enough. Why? Well, you need to look at it from the drum companies' point of view.

Drum companies are there to sell drums. You will need to demonstrate how you can help them do that. Being a great drummer is just not enough unless of course, you are in a big band getting lots of attention. Then, you would be in a position to influence other drummers.

If you have a large student base then that too can help you get endorsed.

In short, the few requirements I have mentioned come down to one requirement. Providing value to the drum company. Just like any job, you would like to have you need to provide a value of some kind to the drum company and because drumming companies basically operate a product-based business you will need to demonstrate that you can help them do that.

At the very least I recommend that if you are interested in pursuing sponsorship that you get your hands on the website forms, I suggested earlier and take a look at the information they want to know about you. This will give you a clue as to what to improve about yourself, your drumming, and ultimately your chance of being accepted.

A good place to begin is at the top. Check out this Yamaha Artist Relations Page which will show you some of the requirements and suggest others.

http://www.yamaha.com/artists/relations.html?CTID=5070090

Oh, and good luck.

Question: Beatles Songs That Have the Best of Ringo's Drumming?
Can you recommend some?

TSD ANSWER: Really, I am not qualified to answer this question but I will have a go...

He's a different type of drummer tied specifically to the era of The Beatles.

He did play for one of the very best composers of our time and just about the biggest band ever.

In truth, I never really rated him as a drummer, but that is basically because I was into the likes of Buddy Rich and Dave Weckl and so on. I was constantly listening to drumming that would stretch my imagination and abilities to the max.

Saying that it's not all about how hard you beat those heads but more about how precisely you do it and how rhythmically as well as tuneful.

John Lennon once made the statement that "he wasn't even the best drummer in the Beatles," However I recently read that when John went out to carve his own solo career, he was supposedly losing his patience with another drummer until John finally flipped and yelled: "Play it as Ringo would!".

Ringo was a great basic drummer. He was lucky enough to have worked with a band that helped get those basic skills to get noticed in a very musical instrument kind of way. By that

I mean he played what needed then some small simple fill or touch that made a massive difference to the end result. He always put the music first. Whether or not that was intentional or due to lack of technical ability I will never know.

I must admit I haven't heard much of his playing in recent years except for the odd Beatles song but he always played exactly what the song required and nothing more. He is a great time player as well as great at creating and keeping the flow going smoothly.

Question: How Can I Get Motivated as A Drummer?

I am learning to play the drums but am not very good at the moment and I am a bit older than your average drummer.

TSD ANSWER: I have seen a few drummers answer this question and most say they look to other drummers, or that a particular drummer motivated them, or that a particular song motivated them.

First, that isn't the way to get motivation. In fact, that isn't motivation at all. It's an influence. And there is a big difference between motivation and influence.

When someone says they were motivated by something that Steve Gadd played or similar what they really mean is that Steve Gadd influenced them to practice something.

Now, what's missing from that last statement. Well, what's missing is the fact that because they practiced the Steve Gadd lick, they became motivated so practiced more.

And that is the secret to motivation. Motivation isn't a cause. It is an effect. Motivation is an effect of ACTION or acting.

Put simply, in order to get motivated to practice more you need to get in the drums and practice more. As you learn and practice motivation kicks in just a little. Then as you practice more, more motivation kicks in, and so on. You have to repeat the action to keep building motivation.

So, when you look to another drummer or another external source of motivation what is really happening is that the source is influencing you to practice. You then get on the drum set and start practicing which kicks the motivation in as you get something right. You play something the right way or it sounded just right. So, you became motivated by your actions.

As you may have noticed within the last paragraph motivation was like a reward to yourself for getting something right. Or playing something well.

So herein lies another secret. To always practice based on a plan. Or a to-do-list of practice areas or subjects. That way, every time you accomplish something you are constantly rewarding yourself with more motivation. At the same time, you instill hope and build hope because the process always accomplishes something.

This is especially true of complex rhythms and systems you may practice. This also eliminates or stops negativity from setting in.

Question: Are You too Old to Learn to Play the Drums or Join A Band?
Within this question, there was mention of both age and the fact that the drummer said he wasn't very good.

I would like to address both of those issues. First, it doesn't matter how old you are, in my opinion. The drummer is always sitting in the back and usually, no one really gets to see him. But that isn't the only reason. If you can play great drums then you are never too old to either start to learn or join a band. If the band members think you are too old for them then they would normally inform you before an audition so it really isn't an issue. Just make sure to inform the band of your age and let them decide.

Now, within the initial question, the drummer also said one statement that you need to remove from your repertoire of words. "I am not that good". If that is how you think then you will constantly struggle against that self-imposed limitation and that subconscious programming. Instead suggest to yourself: Every day in every way I am getting better and better. Speak those words twenty times in the morning and then again twenty times before bed. You can also speak those words throughout the day if you like.

Your words have power and so you should only ever speak and think of yourself in the affirmative.

If you can play the things outlined in parts one and two of the Time Space & Drums Series then start looking in local papers for a band just starting out. Tell them your abilities as well as your age. But remember that in most cases the number one ability they are looking for is a good solid time player.

If the band asks you to try something over a particular part of a song if you can't do it tell them you will work on it for next time and then integrate those little things with your drumming development plan.

Question: Are Electronic Drum Kits OK for a Beginner Drummer to Learn On?

I've played drums before (a long time ago) but am interested in picking it up again. For convenience, an electronic kit would be preferable to an acoustic one. But I am concerned that learning on an electronic kit would influence my touch/feel.

TSD ANSWER: Electronic drums are pretty great, but as the question suggests over time you would need to adjust your playing style if you returned to an acoustic kit.

My acoustic technique went totally out of the window when I moved to electronic kits due to the noise issues, and so I mainly used it with electronics off as simple practice pads/kit. The electronic kits at the time just couldn't handle the intricacies and ghost note as well as dynamics that I like so never really got into or rather mastered them, they are very much about punch it out playing that can be scientifically exact and great but your ears have to adjust when it comes to returning to an acoustic kit.

However, you could learn a lot from them. You could take a deep dive course into the triggering sensitivity settings and sampling etc as well as learning to play them. which could help the end result you get.

Over recent years electronic drums have gotten more controllable regarding speed and sensitivity but I have never personally played those latest models. I do however have a feeling that they would still be far from the acoustic capabilities.

Another thing is the drum heads. When you hit a snare drum, for instance, the head and stick are pretty harsh... yet the electronic manufacturers insist on stating that their mesh heads are very much like the real thing. I have never experienced that to be true.

What I mean exactly is quite complex to explain in words... you really have to try them out to see. But at a basic level (and this doesn't quite make sense although it is true as far as I have experienced) hitting an acoustic snare drum is harsh yet produces a bounce. With the mesh heads, they are only slightly harsh and there is a springiness that causes the bounce. Apologies, but that is the best way I can describe the feeling or the difference.

Saying that I believe the Roland V-drums and their mesh heads have got the best feel of the electronic drumkits available, but they are also pretty expensive.

An electronic drumkit, in general, is an expensive proposition for a beginner because you need to buy all the hardware that is required such as drum pads, rack, sound module, speakers, and the low-end kits will run you about $400-$800.

If I was to start out, I would purchase a low-end electronic kit specifically for practicing and negate the electronics altogether. As a drummer you are really learning mathematical processes which is more about hitting the drum at YOUR required volume. Having the electronics off altogether allows you to do that.

But when you turn on the electronics it is no longer a case of striking one object with a drum stick at whatever volume you dictate as the drummer. It is more about compensating for the delays of what you play and what you hear. And with delays what I am really referring to is the ability of the sound to bend or be formed into what you want to hear. And usually, that gap between what you want to hear and what you actually hear is too great to get comfortable with, in my personal opinion that gap is too large and really affects how you play an acoustic kit.

I actually recorded the Time Space & Drums Series audios using a lower-end Roland kit and had real trouble especially playing the accents throughout the series. I did, however, manage to get everything done with little trouble as at the time I wasn't in the position to be able to use a full acoustic kit. Also, my point was to play scientifically or mathematically over musicality. The musicality can be added as a secondary concern when you get deeper into the technique. But with the Time Space & Drums Series, you have something to work with when that time comes.

Question: I Have Good Speed with My Right Hand but My Left Hand is Really Lacking Speed.

Any tips or techniques on how to improve my left hands' control and speed.

TSD ANSWER: First, the words used in that question tell us a lot. Primarily you used the word speed rather than strength, power, or control. I am sure that you have all three of those with your right hand but not so much with your left hand. So, let's break it right down...

Speed or playing fast whether single or doubles or drumming, in general, is not something you should be focused on at all. Why? Because speed is an effect.

Generally, think about, or use speed like this:

If you can't play something at 60bpm (beats per minute) you won't be able to play it at 70bpm.

That line in itself answers the main question. But it does that by giving you the real answer to the question "why can't I play this fast?" which is, "because you can't play it slow".

And that why you shouldn't be focused on speed at all. Because it is more important to be able to play it slow. The slower the better.

Let me tell you a little story, years ago I used to do local gigs with a really great keyboard player. He used to count a swing-style melody in and we would go. I had to result in playing straight quarter notes to be able to keep up. The traditional swing style beat was simply too fast for me to pull off.

Six months later and I was pushing to play it faster… why? Because I practiced the swing beats and jazz style beats covered in Time Space & Drums Part Two – Jazz drumming Foundation at 60bpm. I never practiced them ay 70, 80 90, 120, or more. I only ever practiced them at 60bpm.

But why did I do this, well at the time I was pushing for better gigs and so needed to get much better and so I thought to myself that if I can't play it at 140bpm then it was because I couldn't play it at 120bpm. And so, if I couldn't play it at 120bpm it was because I couldn't play it at 100bpm and so on.

It then struck me that if I really mastered it at a really slow tempo (and I chose 60bpm) that would give me plenty of time to think. Think about the spaces, think about each note and how I moved physically, think about how the stick hit the drum or cymbal, and then move my focus through each limb.

I then made tiny adjustments as I could see where the issues were. So, I carried on correcting them.

Another thing I did was to instead of focusing on the drumming was to instead focus on reading the exercises, all the time getting better at reading music, all at a slow tempo.

The Martial Art of Drumming
This in effect is exactly what those who practice Tai Chi do. They go through the movements thousands of times really slow but they never practice at speed. Then if someone were to

attack them, they instantly knew the moves to counterattack and render the attacker impotent. Yet they never practiced at speed. Always at a slow meditative tempo.

This all integrates with why I never created videos for the Time Space & Drums Series. Watching videos is not practicing, it is lazy. Watching video attempts to sidestep the hardnosed nitty-gritty study and practice that need doing in order to become great, or simply better.

The main reason for practicing slowly is that you get to deeply understand the movements, the balance, the pulse, and the flow. That deep understanding makes playing faster an effect of mastering it slow. Watching videos is an attempt to get there fast without the effort involved in practice in order to become better.

This is all mainly because we live in a society that seeks instant gratification rather than sacrificing today to become better tomorrow.

In addition to what I have said if your left hand is suffering then you need to go back to the drawing board. Here are some suggestions:

1 - Instead of lifting your cup of coffee with your right hand (if you're right-handed) use your left hand. Try using your left hand for almost everything that you would normally use your right hand for. Of course, avoiding spilling hot coffee or other dangers.

2 - Practice ¼ notes, $1/8^{th}$ notes, then 16th notes just with the weaker hand until you can play them with precision and control at 60bpm, you can then speed up to 70 -90 bpm one increment at a time if you like. This should be done over many weeks in order to really improve. I wouldn't even speed up; I would get it perfect at 60bpm or the absolute slowest tempo you can put up with.

3 - Get yourself a copy of Dave Weckl's first video "Back to Basics" and learn the finger technique. Get the fingers working, at first this will be completely ridiculous until you get used to it but it will also take your focus off of having a slow left hand. Whilst ever you think your left hand is slow it will be slow. Change your thoughts about it.

Question: How Should I Expand A Drum Kit?
My seven-year-old daughter is learning to play drums, she has a basic pearl kit, consisting of... The bass drum (double pedal) snare, 2 toms 1-floor tom 14" ride cymbal 18" crash cymbal, and a hi-hat. She would like to expand her kit. What would you advise her to get?

TSD ANSWER: The short answer it depends on your budget. The longer answer begins by asking other questions:

- What is your budget?
- Is she really going to stick with drumming?
- Do you see her continuing for many years?
- Do you think she will be working in a band soon? If not, when?

You may have other questions to help you decide when and how to expand a drum kit but knowing those answers, and presuming that they were all positive I would instead suggest expanding the drummer.

I don't mean to insult or be too tough as I know that when a youngster gets their eyes on a larger kit it is almost impossible to move them away from it.

You say her basic kit is:

- Bass Drum
- Snare Drum
- High Tom
- Medium Tom
- Low Tom
- 14" Ride Cymbal
- 18" Crash Cymbal
- Hi-hat.

As I suggested rather than expand an existing kit, I would expand the drummer a little more first. Just to make sure that you know she is really going to stick with it. If that is the case then I would replace the whole kit. But I will give you other options so don't worry just yet.

I would increase the kit like this:

- Bass Drum
- Snare Drum
- High Tom
- Medium Tom
- Low Tom
- Low Tom2

- 20" Ride Cymbal
- 10" Splash Cymbal
- 14" Crash Cymbal
- 16" Crash Cymbal

Possibly two snare drums instead of just the one.

However, from the example above you can see the additions that have been made to your current kit. Mainly the addition of an extra floor tom and complete cymbal changeup.

From what I can see the basic Pearl 5-piece kit is already fine and so you may just want to replace the cymbals which will add more color to the existing kit.

I am presuming that you have got a set of upgraded drum heads such as Pin Stripe Heads. I use Pin Stipe Head and A Pearl export Kit for many years and I was able to get an exceptional sound from those drums.

When I did upgrade to a Yamaha 9000R my playing took a boost too as well as the sound got even better.

So, depending on your budget your choices may change.
Adding drums to an existing kit though is in my opinion not the way to go. I would instead replace the drum kit, then upgrade the cymbals.

I would imagine though that from what your existing kit is comprised of that a cymbal upgrade would be required. And so, to upgrade the cymbals you can either get a good, low to medium quality set for around $2-500 or replace one at a time and get better quality cymbals. K Zildjian's for instance.

You would most likely be paying $250 for each cymbal in this case but visiting a local store and making some negotiations could be the answer.

But when you consider my own philosophy of getting things better using the more scientific exacting approach rather than the musical one, she really only needs to add whatever is necessary for the sound she wants to produce.

With a basic 5-piece kit she can probably play or improvise anything she could possibly want to. All that can be expanded on is variety in terms of cymbal and extra's such as cowbells, congas if your Latin Inclined, or add some electronics such as the Roland octopod.

Really, everything depends on the budget which I suspect would depend on the commitment level.

Question: Can You Recommend a Beginner Drummer DVD?

I am a complete beginner and have just bought a drum kit and set it up.
Can you recommend any DVDs for beginners because there are so many out there... something that covers all the basics?

TSD ANSWER: DVDs are great but don't get too caught up in them that you don't get some books, learn to read music, learn some theory and learn more in-depth than a video would normally give.

To the complete beginner, I would always recommend The Time Space & Drums Series as we developed it with the complete beginner in mind. It takes the complete beginner from the very beginning in steps through 12 books and audio demonstrations.

The audio demonstrations are really to give the student an anchor as to what the written exercises sound like. That is because the TSD Series teaches the drummer to learn to read music at the same time. It is essentially a 12-part theory lesson in steps.

So, as I said I would always advise that book series be practiced in steps.

However, I would also recommend the Dave Weckl Back to Basics DVD, in particular, the Snare Drum and Finger Techniques or Rudiments on that same video.

Once the beginner starts to get a grip with those stick-holding techniques and basic rudiments, I would suggest going through the Time Space & Drums Series, one book at a time, and really get to understand the background theory as well as music theory of each part before moving on.

In addition to the TSD Series and the Dave Weckl DVD, I recommend taking at least 12 months' worth of beginner drumming lessons with a private local tutor.

This will give you a great step up the ladder to be able to continue or begin and complete the TSD Series without much trouble. But it is important to not involve your drum teacher with the TSD Series as the series was designed as an addition to whatever you actually decide to do, whether that takes private lessons or learn from books or DVDs

Question: What Does It Really Take to Be A Drummer in A Band?

I know it's not just playing the drums you have to understand music and so on.

TSD ANSWER: Music and drumming are all about TIME & SPACE. What, where, and when you play.

In general, you will need to have a good rock drumming foundation as well as a good jazz drumming foundation. They are the two cornerstones of all drumming and music and each of those integrates (at times) to form a good drummer who can play good time.

Next to that having a more technical foundation in drum fills, phrasing dynamics can only help enhance that foundation.

It is then a case of developing as you gig with the band with a single cause in mind… making the band and music sound better.

When you are on that road it's a good idea to develop a good attitude. A good outlook on life and so on.

That really is it but the better that you implement those things and develop them will determine your success in the end.

I started playing when I was 9 years old and was working in a local band by the time, I was 11. I was working 5 nights per week whilst still at school but all I really knew in regards to actual playing ability was the things I just mentioned. Basic Rock, Basic Jazz, and Basic Rudiments.

From that point on it's a road of never-ending improvement.

But bear in mind that what bass guitarists, keyboard players, and guitarists want as well as the front male or female singer wants is a good solid time player. You are in effect a metronome.

In addition, when you do eventually get better it is a good idea to have some self-discipline so that you don't lay those fancy drum fills you learned in the practice room on the gig. If they do not fit. Just play what is needed, nothing more, and nothing less.

Actually, a good starting point is to be able to play the things that Ringo Starr played with the Beatles songs. It is really a basic level of drumming yet absolutely essential as Ringo obviously knew.

Question: I'm A 16-Year-Old Girl and Want to Play the Drums Professionally for Someone Famous – How Do I Do It?

TSD ANSWER: Well, presuming that you can play the drums already then you need to get better and keep getting better. If you can't read music then learn to. Get the Time Space & Drums Series of books and go through each of them until they are second nature and you have built a good foundation of drumming skills and theories.

That said, you will then need to become acquainted with other musicians in your area if you are not in a band already and get to know them.

Go to your local drum shop and get to know everyone, find out about them and who they play for, and let them know that you are looking for work as a drummer. You may be able to put your contact details on a wall in the store if they have an internal advertising board for musicians.

The shop will also have contacts with every one worth knowing in the local music industry and beyond so befriend them and buy all your drum equipment from them and they will eventually get to know and like you and recommend you when they know of someone looking for a drummer.

Most drum shops will also be able to recommend a good drum teacher who you may want to visit and find out a little more about. Befriending other drummers and teachers can really help you to get your foot in the door of some better-quality bands.

Take lessons from a few teachers to find out what they can teach you and attain as much of their knowledge as you can.

In the end, it is really about befriending the right people which is what Attitude is so important to succeed in anything.

Question: Who Are the Best Drummers in Rock?

TSD ANSWER: I am not really a fan of rock music myself; I find it too... well, heavy. I much prefer the easy life. However, you could check out some of the drummers below who have been known to do some heavy-duty shredding on the kit.

- Steve Smith
- Neil Peart
- John Bonham
- Carl Palmer
- Keith Moon
- Terry Bozzio
- Ginger Baker
- Danny Carey
- Bill Bruford
- Mitch Mitchell
- Alan White
- Gavin Harrison
- Billy Cobham
- Cozy Powell
- Carmine Appice
- Ian Paice
- Charlie Watts

My personal favorite from the above is Steve Smith. He plays or played with the band Journey but my introduction to Steve Smith was as a Jazz Drummer or what you might call contemporary. He is ridiculously great at playing contemporary rock but I have never seen him play really heavy stuff, but that's because I wouldn't listen to it.

I did meet Ian Paice once in Sheffield England at a drum clinic he was performing on in the 90s and he completely blew me away. He played with Deep Purple of course and as an exception, I did listen to the album Made in Japan quite a lot because of the more melodic rock songs in that album.

As for the other drummers, many I have not listened to very much at all with the exception of Steve Smith, Bozzio, Bruford.

Question: How Should I Store My Drums?

TSD ANSWER: Simon Jaye's of The London Drum Company says, "We store around 120 snare drums in our drum warehouse. All of the drums are uncased and always set at a rough playing tension. There is no need to detune anything or slacken any drum lugs off. I would suggest that keeping the drums at the normal tension keeps them in shape and less likely to detune when you do take them out and start playing them again. We always keep the snare strainers on the drums so that the wires don't get damaged in any way and remain flat and true on the head.

The number one golden rule for the storage of drums, cymbals, and hardware is to avoid moisture at any cost. Whether stored in a cool room or a warmer you should make sure the room is not damp and is well ventilated.

If the room is too warm the cover can leave the shell, especially if left in direct sunlight for extended periods so avoid direct heat sources and sunlight at all costs.

It is also a good idea to periodically lubricate the lugs and remove any dust from the shell and chrome, especially around the top of the lugs and rim.

Question: What Do I Need to Play My Electronic Drum Kit Live?

TSD ANSWER: Simply put, it would depend on the band situation and your monitor setup. But as a basic idea, the first thing to consider is what you as the drummer actually hear. With that in mind, you would need some kind of dedicated monitor.

The other thing to consider is that the band leader frontman or sound engineer really has control of your volume and to some extent, the sound as the drums would normally be sent through the main P.A system. Presuming that it was a large rig.

But let's presume that you are speaking from your own personal point of view. As suggested above you would need a good quality high output monitor system either in the form of a wedge monitor that would cost around £600 for a good quality one or a specific drum speaker monitor system.

Yamaha and Roland do quite robust drum amps around the £400-£500 mark. These work pretty well for personal monitoring but as suggested if you can get the sound engineer to pump just the drums through a specific wedge monitor or two and then have monitors for the vocals or rest of the band as normal.

The thing to consider is really having sufficient power at the back end so you can actually hear yourself and the quality of the drum kit over the bassist and those darn guitarists who seem to pay no consideration for your ears. In effect, you are really trying to imitate the sound and volume of an acoustic drum kit.

The cost, weight, and complications of the additional amplification often outweigh any advantages, certainly on smaller gigs which is why my initial reaction was that it depends on the circumstances and size of the gig.

Acoustic drum kits have a far greater dynamic range than an electronic kit which is why good quality and powerful amplification is required to even begin to compete with the dynamic range of an acoustic kit. This is why personal monitoring is so important as the electronic kits can get "lost in music" if you pardon the pun.

Personally, rather than go full-out electronic, a good mid-point is to use drum triggers on the acoustic heads instead. That way all of the above issues become a secondary issue rather than the main issue. Of course, it would also depend if the acoustic kit was miked up in the first place.

Question: Should I polish my cymbals?

TSD ANSWER: I have seen many answers to this question and most I completely disagree with. Here are some examples:

Symbols don't sound the same after you have cleaned them

It would depend on what look you prefer?

Some bands have an ultra-clean stage presentation so having clean cymbals is important. Clean them!

For some more casual bands the grungier and funkier the better. Don't clean them! Some fastidious drummers may go as far as to use soft cotton gloves to pick up cymbals by their edges, wipe any marks off with a soft dry cloth and keep them in protective bags to make sure they stay clean.

A duller-looking cymbal may actually sound slightly less toppy. So, I don't clean them.

There are many other similar answers given to this question but in my own experience, I have always kept a clean kit and symbols. Every 3-6 months I would strip each drum down to the bare shell and clean every piece of chrome individually.

When it comes to the cymbals, I always used either Brasso or Brilliantine. I was always told to never use such harsh abrasive materials but I never had any issues. My cymbals always sounded great to me.

When I look at it logically the very tiny microscopic layer of metal that was removed from the cymbal (if any) made absolutely no difference to the sound at all. In fact, one of the remarks about duller cymbals sounding less toppy mentioned above was actually the opposite of what I experienced.

After cleaning the cymbals, I found that they sounded a little dull. But after 10 minutes I realized that this was all psychological and the cymbals soon began to sound great again.

I believe it is a myth that cleaning cymbals will spoil the sound. But hey, I'm the drummer, I'm not very good with authority!

You just have to rub the dark Brasso marks off fast so the Brasso doesn't dry into the grooves of the cymbals. I then rubbed a much cleaner cloth around the grooves in a circular motion around the circumference of the cymbal. Oh, and always use a soft cloth to apply and polish the cymbals clean.

Question: How Do I Stop My Bass Drum and Hi-hat Pedals Creeping?

TSD ANSWER: Many bass drums and hi-hat pedals have toe-stops fitted to counteract the problem, but in my own experience they never do a great job unless you hammer them into the wooden stage.

To get around the issue myself before the newer drum mats became available (I have never used them as my solution worked for me) I set my kit up on a square carpet. Here are the exact procedures and you can change and adapt them to suit your own kit.

Cut a piece of carpet square around your kit. I always visited the carpet store and purchased one of the odd bits that would do the trick in a darker color as possible.

I then got a series of wooden lattes around the kit. One in front of the bass drum (24" long), one in front of the hi-hat tripod legs (18" long), and a few others mainly one to the left of the kit and one to the right that stopped any other cymbal stands sliding through vibrations and so on.

I marked out with a black marker the outside edge of each of the wooden lattes and marked the edges too.

I then removed the carpet from underneath the kit.

Then I got some large thin metal discs. And drilled a single hole in the center of each.

Then from the bottom/underside of the carpet, I screwed 4 screws (with the metal washers I made) into each piece of wood. (I drilled the wood first because the type of wood I used was hardwood and not soft pine wood or any other softwood).

That mostly did the trick except that I sometimes had issues with the actual drum stool moving too so you could also add lattes around the stool area.

However, under most circumstances, I used to just carry a simple piece of foam-backed carpet and used that on wooden stages. If the stage was carpeted, I would still use my own carpet.

If I was doing a residency at any particular theatre or hotel or seasonal job, I would actually screw the wooden lattes to the stage. Presuming that it wasn't a shiny wooden stage but most of my gigs were on specifically designed drum risers in the orchestra pit and so on so this wasn't much of a problem.

In my earlier day in bands, it was quite a problem and I would always use my discretion and carry a couple of lattes around with me and would screw them to the stage … if I wasn't going to destroy a brand-new shiny floor. I would only do this on stages that were very worn or slightly damaged and never on a high-quality stage and I didn't do it on a regular basis as it was just a backup plan for my existing carpet trick.

Question: Why Should I Cut A Hole in My Bass Drum Head?

TSD ANSWER: This is a tricky yet simple question to answer. First the tricky answer:

In the 60s and 70s, many drummers remove the front head altogether and used lots of damping to cope with multiple mikes and close miking.

By the time the 80s came around drummers began to cut a hole in the front head instead.

Deep Purple's Ian Paice says: "there are many points to consider with bass drum tuning, damping and miking. First, the only time you cut a hole in the front head is for using a microphone. Acoustically, a bass drum sounds best with two complete heads. This gives depth, duration of note, and warmth - which the microphone really doesn't like! Personally,

I love the 'old school' sound of a bass drum (with complete heads), but I do understand that in modern amplified music it often will not work as well as a 'doctored', miked-up drum.

Bigger drums require you to use more internal muffling to eradicate the overtones that are inherent in the drum.

The bass drum beater is also very important as if you choose a beater that is too soft you lose impact or attack but if the beater is a hard-wooden beater or plastic you lose depth. I always prefer the hard-felt beaters which give me the attack I want yet produces a deep warmer sound.

I have never used the larger 24" drums as I understood that they would require more damping to get a good sound and that didn't appeal to me personally. I have fewer problems using a 22" but it could still be a bit troublesome. However, when I moved down to a 20" bass drum the sound was much more constant.

The simpler answer is that you should cut a circle on your front drum head to be able to move the muffling around to change the dampening level.

I always cut a 12" hole in the drum head for one reason only. To be able to slightly move the soft pillow I had stuffed in there either away from the beater side or onto it slightly more depending on the room size and furnishings.

The pillow was always touching the front head too to stop the ringing and produce a deeper deader and much warmer sound. On rare occasions, I added a little gaffer tape to the backside of the front head. This was to stop any flutter of the drum head around the cut-out.

Oh, the cut-out circle was also useful for miking the kit up should the need arise on larger gigs.

Question: Can I Fix My Broken Cymbals?

TSD ANSWER: In a word... no. I say that based on experience and by asking other questions that arise. First, if you have broken cymbals you are hitting them wrong, or they are low-quality cymbals and are not worth fixing. It's better just to replace them with better quality cymbals.

Second, if you are hitting them wrong and therefore breaking them, you need to note a couple of things. 1 - By hitting a cymbal harder it only has a certain volume and hitting it harder won't make any difference to the volume. 2 - The cymbal has a specific individual sound; it is an instrument and not a trash can lid.

Therefore, it has a specific sound that is found by striking the cymbal on the edge (presuming it's a crash) and not hitting INTO the cymbal but rather gliding across the circumference in a circular motion. Kind of an in-and-out sweeping motion rather than a simple INTO as ferociously as possible. It is really just a glancing blow and not a direct striking. That way the cymbal produces ITS sound, not the one you are trying to get from it? And it's important not to over-tighten the wing nut too - allow the cymbal to sway loosely.

Question: How Should I Tune My Resonant Heads?

TSD ANSWER: Resonant heads are so-called because the purpose is to maximize the resonance of the sound of the drum when tensioned sympathetically in relation to the batter side drum heads.

I have heard drummers say that the batter head creates the feel and attack while the resonance head produces the projection, tone, and sustain.

In its most simple form, I always detune both heads and then bring them both up in tension just to the point of removing all of the wrinkles in the side near the rims. The heads are now seated pretty well. I then take the resonant head up in tension about half a turn for each lug nut then I concentrate solely on the batter head and tune the drum to get the basic tone that I want. It is simply a case of adjusting the drum to get the sound I want. That adjustment may require the resonant head to be slackened off a touch or increased tension just a touch.

The important thing for me specifically is I try to get the drum to produce its natural sound. Following the above procedure, it usually does produce a natural sound close to what the drum was designed to produce.

When I make the final adjustments, I may just slacken off a single lug nut, or indeed may increase the tension of a single lug nut. This is because I like a natural sound yet prefer as little ring as possible in favor of a very slight boom or bend.

Sometimes instead of increasing an individual nut, I may just add a little gaffer tape to that one area of the drum. Even on the bottom heads. I do this because in most cases I am being miked up and prefer a dead sound with a slight boom. I add gaffer tape because I want complete control of the length of that boom.

So apart from having slightly more tension, I do tune both heads the same. Then make the final sound adjustment. To do this you may want to remember the starting point of the lug you're altering in order to return it to its starting point should you not get the sound you were looking for.

It's natural to tension your top head so it feels great where you are sitting too, so it can be a shock when you go out into the room and listen to someone else playing your drums.

To compensate for any issues out in the room I always hold the drum at arm's length and turn away from it then strike it to see if it produces the sound I want from a short distance. This actually sounds crazy as I write it but it does actually work for me. Removing yourself from the immediate environment of the drum to 3-4 feet away is all that I need to know that the drum will usually sound great.

An important point when I do all this is to do it all with the room in mind., What are the furnishings, mostly wood or mostly curtain and carpet. That makes a big difference to the sound.

I usually use pinstripes on the batter heads because I like the depth and crisp sound they produce on the toms. On the resonant heads, I prefer clear Ambassador heads. I prefer the coated head on the snare drum.

Top session drummer Ralph Salmins says: "I usually derive more pitch from the bottom head. Once the heads are seated, I try to get both approximately the same pitch, whether tuning high or low. This gives a clean, resonant decay. Try to find the pitch of the drum that seems most natural to you. I find this is often not too high but closer to the bottom end of the tuning range.

As far as heads go... I prefer a Clear Ambassador resonant and Coated Ambassador batter. I use Coated Emperors on floor toms for a little extra fatness".

"I take the drums off their mounts and tune the bottom heads if I'm not getting the sound I want. A pain, but it has to be done – this really affects the whole sound. I only change bottom heads when they are worn out… every few years probably. Fresh ones always make a difference of course."

Question: What's the Best Way to Tame Snare Drum Buzz?

TSD ANSWER: In all honesty, I did have this issue when I first started out but have never really had this problem enough to be qualified in solving it.

All I can do is suggest that you tune the snare drum the same as I tune the drums as described in the previous question.

After that, there are a couple of things to consider. First, I like my snare top to be tuned really tight. After that, I may detune it slightly just to get a deeper sound to the tight crispness.

Regarding the bottom head, I always tune it as high as possible. Then when I hold the snare and strike it floating in the air the snares don't usually buzz very much at all. On the odd occasion that they do buzz, I tighten the 4 lugs near where the snares are attached.

I believe that the tighter the head the less buzz occurs due to the heads vibrating much less.

After getting to this stage, I may add a small piece of gaffer tape to the batter head to stop any overtones that I don't like. Bearing in mind the room and the furnishings again.

When you do get over buzz it is usually due to a ringing nearby tom or a nearby bass speaker. I always try to remove both from the immediate environment of the snare drum. I would never set the kit up in a band situation where the snare drum was in front of the bass speaker. Always parallel with it.

When I had the buzz issues early in my playing, I believe it was mainly due to lower quality drums and head. I like the snares to be tight to so that may be the main rea=son that I haven't had much trouble with snare buzz in many years.

If it's a nearby tom causing the buzz a small adjustment in the tom, or as suggested slightly tightening the tension lug nuts on either side of the snare wires can often alleviate the problem.

If you are being miked up then using top head overhead mikes rather than mikes below the snare drum can also help. It just depends on the situation as to possible solutions.

In my early days, I actually used to add a little gaffer tape to the snares themselves. How much of course depends on what you are willing to put up with regarding the amount of buzz. I was very inexperienced at the time but it did do the job. However, when my playing, knowledge, and experience tuning and setting up developed... the buzz began to subside.

Saying all of that, I do like a little buzz simply because that is the purpose of the snare drum in the first place but using the ideas above, I was able to control the amount of buzz I was willing to put up with and wanted.

Question: What's the Secret to A Low, Booming Bass Drum Sound?

TSD ANSWER: Usually as a drummer you will find your own way of tuning your specific sized drums the way you like them through constant experimentation. What this question refers to I prefer to call deep with a little bend.

However, in general, the larger the drum the more the boom. The more the padding or muffling of that drum the less the boom.

Over more recent years drummers have begun using close mikes to each drum head and so boom has, in general, become an undesirable element of a drum's sound. Simply because when amplified through a large P.A. system the boom overrides the other instruments and just gets in the way. And so, controlling the amount of boom is essential whatever your situation.

Again, regarding the boom or bend as I prefer to call it due to my tuning of the resonant heads slightly tighter than the batter heads, I prefer to think about it backward. For example, after tuning the drum and getting the tone I like I usually dampen the batter head a lot. This helps me to hear the ring from the resonant head and the tone it will be... booming out. I then detune or increase the resonant head to the tone I like.

After which I remove more and more dampening of the batter head until I get the right amount of dampening. At this point, I have usually achieved a good level of the bend. This is achieved by also touching the resonant head slightly with the inner dampening of the bass drum but only very slight.

To increase to ring or boom then I would just remove more and more dampening from both heads.

Cutting a hole in the front resonant head along with putting damping inside the drum and using heads that have damping elements built-in, or the double-ply type heads such as some of the Evans Blue Heads or Remo Pinstripe heads, all these individual elements reduce the boom and help control the sound.

Baring all of that in mind I have never played anything above 22-inch bass drums. That's because I don't like the booming ring of the larger drums. I moved from a 22-inch bass drum many years ago and used a 20x20 which provided loads of bend for me personally.

Question: What's the Difference Between Wooden, Steel, and Synthetic Drum Shells?

TSD ANSWER: This is a question that I am going to pass onto someone else to answer as I have had very little experience in a variety of shell types.

But before I pass it on, I will add my experiences as they may influence you to make choices that will improve your drum sound and drumming so here goes.

I have a friend who many years ago gave me a drumming lesson on his Ludwig Vistalite kit. The toms and bass drum were Vistalite and the snare drum was steel. He had blue Evens oil-filled heads on the toms and bass drum and the sound that kit made will stick with me for the rest of my life. The toms and bass drum were completely awesome. They sounded like Steve Gadd-type drums recorded in the best studio. All of that was in a small living area.

For many years I tried to reproduce that sound with the kits I had but couldn't get anywhere near it.

I concluded that it was my tuning and not the kit at all. Although it was probably the kit to a large extent.

Over the years of experimenting, I always found birch to be the choice for me when it comes to toms and bass drums. But I could never get on with wooden snare drums. I like high-pitched cracks and not deep warm sounds from the snare so steel was a better choice for me.

Then when Yamaha produced the Piccolo snare drum, I couldn't play any other snare drum. I fell in love with it and the tight crisp sound it produced that was also warm.

That is as far as my own experience with different shell materials go and so I now refer you

to Carl Palmer on the same subject. Bear in mind though that Carl Palmer is as far as I know a pretty heavy hitter.

He has though, explored different drum materials more than just about anybody and he says, *"for me, the problem with wood has been this 'cosy', warm, almost passionate sound! Great for jazz/big band and some types of rock. Because many species of wood are used this argument does not always apply.*

For example, I have a Brady set in Jarrah ply, the best wooden drums I have ever played. The sound is full, loud, deep, and clear. Jarrah can sustain 1,800 psi (pounds per square inch) of shell pressure.

Tuning is very good in the low register but gets harder in the high area, say a 12"x8" tom. To get the top end clear and bright you may need a thinner-gauge head, say an Ambassador rather than an Emperor.

This wood offers very good sound projection on all levels – only the head configuration needs to be considered to gain a wide range of tuning. This cannot be said for lots of other woods that are still being used to manufacture drums."

"Stainless steel is my personal favorite," continues Carl, *"because the sound projection in most conditions is extremely good – clear, loud, and fast response.*

Great for prog rock! The top-end brightness is very good and the sound seems to pass through the shell very quickly – there is no [wood] grain, vertical or horizontal, to deal with. So, you have an added advantage when playing the toms in any detailed way, as toms always respond slower.

"Stainless steel comes into its own regarding tom projection overall. Tuning is absolutely perfect in all areas of the pitch – quick and easy. Bass drums have an extremely wide range of depth. The set I play was made for me to celebrate Ludwig's 100th Anniversary."

"Perspex is not as loud as stainless steel but has some similarities in the projection and tuning. The Blue Ludwig Vistalite set that I have in Europe has always sounded good straight

out of the cases and the new welds used in the shell construction make tuning a lot better and quicker.

The drums retain their sound overall throughout a concert. They are not as loud as some wood drums but are very clean-sounding. And the heavier the head, say, an Emperor or CS Black Dot, the better the sound overall. Because the low-end on these drums takes some time to get on the smaller sizes it is down to tuning the drum how you like it and hitting it harder for projection.

The drums sound inspirational when you are behind them, but from out front, it is a lighter sound overall. But these drums have a certain magic when you record them. The floor toms can sound fantastic."

Question: Can I Learn to Play the Drums Without a Drum Kit?

TSD ANSWER: In a word, yes. You can make a good start that can actually be beneficial. My book Modern Drumming Concepts explains in more detail but here are the nuts and bolts you may want to consider:

Buy a pair of sticks and use a hard pillow to learn basic drum rudiments. Learn to visualize yourself at a real drum kit and go through the Time Space & Drums Series as they are centered around hearing a beat and seeing the beat written down. You can go on for many months through the whole series learning the theory and the movements involved.

It may be more difficult to get motivated but if you have the discipline to follow the above advice, when you eventually get a drum kit would make the transition pretty quickly.

In the end, drumming is about knowledge and theory so learning the theory of drumming and reading music as in the Time Space & Drums Series will stand you in very good stead for when you decide to buy a full drum kit.

Question: When Should A Drummer Who Is Just Starting Out Get a Drum Kit?

TSD ANSWER: Although it will take more discipline, I believe a good knowledge base is a good place to start learning to play the drums. Time Space & Drums have produced several free books that you might want to start reading and to do so a few times until you fully understand the theory.

If you review the last question, I made some specific suggestions regarding getting started practicing. And again, Modern Drumming Concepts gives some very good tips on getting started as well as improving your drumming many of which do not require a drum kit to get started.

Self-discipline is key as this can be a very good route to take it does take discipline to stick to and know that you will be getting value from it.

I stated that visualizing playing a real kit in the previous question can be very powerful. Stanford University has conducted tests that prove that the brain doesn't know the difference between playing a drum beat and imagining playing the drumbeat. The improvement of the drummer can be just as good as if you were actually playing a real drum kit.

Imagination is also a very powerful tool that many drummers can come to lack simply because it takes lots of self-discipline. See Modern Drumming Concepts for more in-depth details.

You can also take lessons and explain to the teacher that you don't have a kit yet and that you are going to discipline yourself to practice this stuff. He will most likely be very impressed.

If you persist with this for 6 months you absolutely deserve a real drum kit. Even though this method will have served you very well and so should continue to improve the imaginative ability.

Question: Where's the Best Place to Buy Drums?

TSD ANSWER: The best option for beginner's drum kits is most probably a good local music shop. When you buy from a local store you can always refer back to them if you need any assistance or have any problems with the drum kit.

You should also note that beginner drum kits are so cheap to buy new that you're not going to save a great deal by buying second-hand. That is unless you prefer to buy a mid-range or higher range kit rather than a lower quality new one. You need to research different sources if this is your preference.

You can search in your local second-hand stores, charity shops as well as local online marketplaces such as eBay or Gumtree. Although I have never used it Craigslist is still going strong as far as I know so you could check there too for the nearest local sources.

Question: How High Should I Setup My Snare Drum, Tom, and Cymbals?

TSD ANSWER: The simple answer to this is to first sit at your drum kit and adjust the height of the snared drum so that when you place your feet on the pedals and lift your heels off of the ground or pedalboard approximately 1 inch, that your thighs or upper legs are parallel with the ground. This is the basic seating position.

You should then set up your snare drum so that as you sit relaxed with your forearms parallel with the ground holding the stick... the stick should be straight out and resting at the center of the snare drum head. You may want to have the snare drum slanting in towards you.

The rest of the kit, toms, and cymbals should all be within easy reach without expending too much effort. You shouldn't set the cymbals up so that they look cool. Set them up so they require as little movement as possible to reach.

Just make sure you are comfortable and can reach everything easily and don't have to spend too much energy or time reaching for a particular drum or cymbal.

Question: I'm Left-Handed - Do I Set My Drums Up Differently?

TSD ANSWER: Most left-handed drummers do set their drums up opposite to right-handed players, e.g., snare and hi-hat on the right-hand side and floor - tom and ride cymbal on the left.

However, some left-handed drummers do prefer to keep the drums set up as a right-handed kit.

They then play their basic beats open-armed or put another way they don't cross the right hand over the left hand to play the hi-hats. They then have the ride cymbal on the left side too in the same position a crash cymbal would usually be in.

They are in effect then playing the bass drum with the right foot which makes them both left and right-handed.

I do recommend that left-hand players start by setting the kit up right-handed then see what seems most awkward. They can then try setting the kit up as a left-handed player with everything the opposite way around and try playing on a left-handed kit to see if that is more comfortable to them.

If they discovered that it is more comfortable to play both hands on a left-handed kit, but the pedals are more comfortably played on a right-handed kit then you simply create a kit with right-hand pedals, hi-hat, and bass drum and then set the top half of the kit as a left-handed kit.

In the end, left-hand drummers will have to experiment to see what works best for them, and then as they begin to learn the basic drum beats and fills move things around until the most comfortable positions are found. In this case, it may take some time until you learn the basic beats and fills and get comfortable playing those beats before changing things around to see if a better option is available to you.

I am completely right-handed and I know some right-handed people play left-handed golf which is completely alien to me so again I cannot offer an exact option as it seems most people can be a mixture of both at specific times.

The main thing is to realize that you can set things up as you like and the kit doesn't necessarily need to be either left-handed or right-handed. But only with a little experimentation will you come to discover what is best for you.

In the beginning, until you have learned and practiced the first few basic beats and drum fills it would probably serve the left-handed drummer to set the kit up left-handed, and then try the above pointers when you feel comfortable playing the basic beats and fills.

Question: Can I Teach Myself to Play the Drums or Do I Need A Professional Drum Teacher?

TSD ANSWER: I asked myself this question before I began writing the Time Space & Drums Series. I imagined a complete beginner and went through everything that the drummer would learn if he did go to a good teacher. Including: setting the drums up, sitting at the kit and correct posture, foot positions on the pedals, holding the sticks, hitting the drums, then the first drum beats. The Time Space & Drums Series is the effect of that process.

And so, yes you can learn to play the drums by yourself and as suggested that is what the Time Space & Drums Series does. It takes you through the whole process of learning. At the same time learning the beginner to understand drum charts and read music.

Many great drummers were self-taught but you really have to ask the question, "what does self-taught mean?" Does it mean you learn from no other drummers at all, music, books, or videos? No, it means you never get a teacher to show you the way, one-on-one which is almost impossible as most so-called self-taught drummer listened to other drummers, read many books, and watched a few videos along the way.

The important thing to take on board at the beginning is that the whole process of learning to play drums would be much simpler if you had some background theory under your belt first. And by that, I mean knowledge of music theory, notation, and a good understanding of the basic requirements of a drummer.

To that end, I am in the process of developing a collection of supplemental drumming theory books. They cover some very basic background and theoretical concepts useful when you are just starting out. There's even a book called "Getting the Gig" which is a book about auditioning for drumming jobs and interviewing techniques.

After those supplemental books as well as this one you can take the theory a little further through the main 4 foundational books available in the series. These are:

Rock Drumming Foundation Course (Book 1)
Jazz Drumming Foundation Course (Book 2)
Odd Time Drumming Development Course (Book 5)
Basic Latin Drumming Foundation Course (Book 8)

These books cover all the most basic drumming foundation skills and theories that will stand you in good stead should you decide to then begin building your skills either by continuing the Time Space & Drums Series of Books, taking Private One-on-One Drum Lessons, or Both.

Whichever route you choose it is also important to understand that a teacher is a means to an end. That end is learning and improving your drumming, this is covered more fully in Modern Drumming Concepts which is supplemental to the Time Space & Drums Series.

Question: How Do I Find & Choose A Drum Teacher?

TSD ANSWER: The first place I would look for a drum teacher is within your local free newspapers to see if anyone is advertising there. If not, then the best option is to visit a local music store. Usually, most of the good musical instrument stores will have a drum department that you can visit to make inquiries.

The drum store may have a dedicated drum tutor or may be able to recommend someone to you in your local area.

It's a good idea to take a free lesson if there is one available or at least take a single short lesson to find out more about the teacher and what areas they specialize in if any. This comes into play more as you develop as a drummer and so, in the beginning, it is more important that you get on well with the teacher and he can show you the basics.

These first steps are initially to get you started and so just about any drum tutor will be able to do that. I do strongly advise that alongside whichever tutor you choose to follow the Time Space & Drums program as well as it was created with the beginner in mind and will help you to get a good hold of the foundational basics. Maybe even before you take your first lesson, especially in regards to the background theory that will more than likely crop up at the tutors.

That way you are not wasting the precious lesson time because you don't understand something he says.

Don't be afraid to ask the teacher what their background in music and drumming is, how long they've been playing, and how long they've been teaching drums.

In music education you generally get what you pay for - cheap drum lessons are not always the best route but they can help you get started which is more important than a great teacher in the beginning stages.

Many won't agree with that statement but as I suggested earlier if you can do it alone from books you can also do it alone from books alongside a reasonably good teacher.

I actually don't believe in the concept of a bad teacher as everyone has something that they can teach, even if it is just how to hold the sticks, sit at the kit and play a basic beat. It all depends on what you want to specifically learn from the teacher in question.

Everything from that point onwards is about how hard you the student are willing to learn and practice and not so much about how great the drum teacher is.

In the end, you get what you pay for and the really great teachers won't even be available to the complete beginner who is just starting out as the price would be many times that of a £20 per hour teacher, maybe even thousands.

So, the reasonably good to the very good teacher along with reading drum exercise books could be the way to go until you want to travel further to find a better teacher who is more experienced in a specific style that you want to learn.

If you have the books and a reasonable teacher then you are most likely dealing with someone who has more than likely had a long background in drumming so must inevitably know what they are talking about.

In the beginning, it is more important to just get started. You can then try a variety of teachers and see which suits you best.

I have followed a single rule in the past though whenever I have taken lessons. If what I want to learn from a new teacher is way beyond me at that moment, I would normally buy a basic book on the subject and practice it so that my time with the teacher was better spent as I had prepared for a week or month or two in advance.

Question: How Often Should I Be Practising the Drums?

TSD ANSWER: Depending on the level you aspire to and the degree of mastery you want to achieve will determine the amount of practice time you spend.

I use the word spend very specifically because, in the end, you will be spending your time. Think of it as you would money. The time you spend practicing should, therefore, be planned out to a schedule so as not to be wasted. Have specific goals.

If I may return to the Time Space & Drums Series for a moment, I will give you an example to replicate.

The Time Space & Drums Series is a 12-part program. Depending on your level of skill the twelve parts can be each practiced in 6 weeks, as there are fundamentally six lessons in each part. So, one lesson a week will take you through the whole process.

If on the other hand, you have had some playing experience that time will be shortened and each book may just take a single week to master all six lessons.

The point I am getting at is that the series is a set of 12 drumming goals that are planned out before you. The amount of time that you apply to that learning and practicing process is individual and as suggested determined by how good you want to be.

As a benchmark, I would suggest practicing at least 30 minutes per day just playing rudiments and another 30 minutes per day practicing at the kit.

Again, if that is too much for you, you may wish to half that time. Or indeed, you may want to double it. In the end, the better you want to be the more you will need to practice.

Most teachers will suggest, that you at least practice every day even if it is just half an hour per day. This is fine so long as you are not concerned with really getting good. But if you are, then I believe in the beginning you can afford to practice one day on and one day off for an hour or two and possibly more each session.

The point of this is that in the beginning, you would be better off having 2 or more hours of practice and then taking a day off because when you return to the kit you will begin to build muscle memory more deeply as you go, simply because your longer practice session programmed more in.

True you would do the same having half-hour per day but I believe small binge practice sessions of 2-4 hours per day is better in the beginning… at least for the first few months until the basics get ingrained in your memories.

Then at that point, it becomes more important to practice on a regular basis.

Whether you practice half an hour, one hour, or more each day is up to you and your progress will help you determine the amount of time you want to put in, again depending on the degree of mastery you want to achieve.

Another thing to bear in mind is that it is important to have plenty of short breaks. Stand up and walk around, stretch and then return to the kit after a few minutes. This is because more is learned in the beginning and at the end of study or practice so it's important to have lots of ends and beginnings to your routine.

You should be taking a two-minute break every 15-20 minutes to take advantage of this accelerated learning strategy.

There has been much said that you must enjoy what you are doing more than disciplining yourself but I believe that to be complete nonsense. In the beginning, it is more important to discipline yourself, and then as you develop you will enjoy your practice sessions more and more.

But it is my personal opinion that we only really enjoy something that we are good at. So, put self-discipline above having fun, to begin with. And never let the fun of it, stop the development. Presuming of course that you want to improve?

Question: What Should I Practice?

TSD ANSWER: There is an important quality that is required to answer this question fully and that I suggested in the last question. That quality is self-discipline. Self-discipline is the maker and breaker of great drummers, great guitarists, and greatness in general. It is so vitally important that I created a whole program around the subject of self-discipline.

That said, to answer the question... you should always practice things that you cannot play yet. You should always favor practicing new things over what you already know otherwise you won't be constantly developing. That takes self-discipline to keep pushing forward and learning new things rather than practicing things you already know.

In that last statement, I separated learning from practice because when you are trying something new such as complex independence exercises you are really learning new things. The practice of that thing comes in when your muscle memory has made the adjustment and can now play that more complex combination.

You then practice the complex independence exercise until you have it mastered... then move onto something new.

That answer is given as a default strategy to follow as you develop but in a more practical sense as you are first starting out it would be a good idea to again follow the subjects within the Time Space & Drums Series. You can view them on Amazon or your favorite book store

And at the same time practice the main rudiments. Singles, doubles, paradiddles, triplets, closed roll, flams, and drags... as well as a few more that are included throughout the TSD Series. They are added in a progressive manner.
You can then practice reading exercises and song charts as you develop.

Question: Do I Need to Read Music to Play the Drums?

TSD ANSWER: There is only one answer to this question but in reality, there are really two answers to this question.

The one answer is this: Yes absolutely. Why? Let's take a look. Drumming at its most fundamental is all about rhythms and time. Or, put another way, what you play and where you play it. In that music is really a mathematical process of rhythms, which is the main feature of most classical music. The music is played mathematically exact and of course, the tones used are exact.

As a drummer, it should be, and I say should be because people do ask this question and it seems in most part to take a shortcut or if they are genuinely interested, they ask the question to confirm to themselves that they should be reading music as part of their learning.

So where does reading music come in as a drummer?
For the most part, there are two possibilities. Being able to read music will help with music reading gigs that you may aspire to play on. If you do not want to play the type of gigs that require you to read music such as in pop bands, rock bands, and so on... then, for the most part, you don't have to read music.

That said as a reader myself whenever I was called upon to learn a band set or individual songs, I would write a drum chart. This process is covered in Time Space & Drums Part 6 - Space to Play so I won't go into it here.

In a band situation if there are no drum charts then writing one yourself as a process of learning the song where you can add specific drum fills of your own or taken from the original song is a great idea as it lets both yourself and the other band members hear what a song is going to sound like when it develops. Plus, they get to hear the full song in a shorter time as possible.

However, if you don't want to learn how to read music then you don't have to unless as suggested you plan to play on gigs that require you to read such as theatre gigs, some club job sessions, and or recording sessions.

Question: So Why Do People Learn to Read Music?

TSD ANSWER: I just covered this in the last question but generally for the same reason people learn how to read words: It greatly increases your ability to communicate with other band members and musicians and it also speeds up the learning process as mentioned in the last question.

Reading music also allows you to forget about the theoretical part when going through practice exercises in books and so you can concentrate on playing the exercises with as much precision as possible.

Question: Is Learning to Read Music Hard?

TSD ANSWER: Drumming as suggested is a mathematical process that requires you to mainly understand 'note value's and then to interpret them exactly as they are written. It is really that simple, but with the addition of a few Musical Symbols, you need to memorize along with a few Musical Terms to learn. So, the short answer is that music is not really that difficult to learn. At its basic level, a drum chart is simply a map of the whole song made up of the notes and dynamics that are given through the musical terms and symbols.

Time Space & Drums Offer a free book containing The Most Popular Musical Terms. Just register to download it for free.

Question: How Can I Make My Drums Quieter?

TSD ANSWER: There are a few options available that may help here depending on the reason you want to dampen the drums down. First, if it because they are too loud for you personally as you play them then you can simply use earplugs or headphones when you play.

On the other hand, if this is because of the neighbors within the same building or adjacent to your home then you can begin by soundproofing the room. But remember here that sound vibrates and it is not necessarily the physical volume of the drums so begin by placing the kit on a thick carpeted area that is as thick as possible yet doesn't cause the snare drum and cymbal stands to wobble.

Soundproofing really helps with the vibration... if you have wooden floors and walls then you need to soften the materials by using curtains and carpets instead of blinds and wooden floors. There are special foams that you can get for the walls.

The second stage would be to dampen the kit down as much as possible. If applying a simple strip of gaffer tape to the head's top and bottom isn't enough then you may want to look into practice pads to place on the heads.

Beyond that, if you still have problems it's really about time to get a dedicated practice kit and leave the kit playing for gigs.

I really enjoyed this process as I built a practice kit from wood myself and glued rubber pads to the tops and added my hi-hat with an old tea towel hung over the top.

Of course, this didn't sound great but as previously suggested drumming is a mathematical process first and foremost and so this helped me really to practice my swing beats and more complex straight-ahead rock-type rhythms in a mathematical way along with a metronome. Doing this I found that my playing on the gigs that I would do was getting better and better as I was more likely to discipline myself and develop.

Failing that you could go for a cheaper electronic kit and use that to practice or replace an actual practice kit made from wood or other material.

Question: Can You Learn to Play Drums on An Electronic Kit?

TSD ANSWER: As I have already suggested in the last few questions practice kits or electronic kits can be good to get the mathematical movements down. But I say that based on playing the electronic kit as a practice kit and not an electronic kit.

Electronics as already mentioned cause what you might call a delay AFTER playing an acoustic kit because you are always trying to create an acoustic kit sound.

Although the advances in electronic drums have been great over the years, I don't think that they will ever replace an acoustic kit. The gap is just too wide regarding the dynamics which is what you are better to practice with the electronic kit off and just use the pads for mathematical exactness in your playing. You will also get the full range of dynamics back that having the electronics switched on takes away.

So yes, you can learn on them but suggest you have the electronic side switched off.

As I said previously, I recorded the audio demonstrations for the Time Space & Drums Series on an electronic kit and had a lot of difficulties getting the dynamic right. Possibly because I never really liked them but at the time it was the only option for me.

Question: Would You Recommend Electronic Drums?

TSD ANSWER: I would only advise an electronic kit to drummers who couldn't practice on an acoustic kit. As previously suggested, I advise using them as a practice kit only. Unless you want to really master the triggering mechanisms and work on the dynamics and sensitivities but I myself could never get them to play nice, but I was trying to reproduce an acoustic sound which of course they never could. Speaking dynamically that is.

So only go electronic if you absolutely have to or in addition to an acoustic kit.

Time Space & Drums Specific Questions

Question: Do I Have to Live in A Specific Area to Start the Course?

TSD ANSWER: No, the course materials are written in English so can be used by any English-speaking person. Anywhere in the world.

Question: Can You Explain the Price of The Course, It Seems a Little Expensive?

TSD ANSWER: The Time Space & Drums Series is a complete foundational development program and were specifically designed as a start to finish *(there isn't really an end to study of any kind unless you choose)* step-by-step process enabling you to build a solid foundation of skills you could build on throughout your drumming lifetime.

The series teaches how to play the drums but also guides the beginner and intermediate players (with a few tricks for the advanced player) down the road to greater success.

We cover just about every facet of learning how to play the drums plus a whole lot more. In short, this is more than just a drum lesson series, program, or course. It's an opportunity for you to become a teacher.

Question: Do You Offer Private One-On-One Drum Lessons?

TSD ANSWER: No, the series materials are written in English so can be used by any English-speaking person. Anywhere in the world. Apart from the main series of books the Time Space & Drums Series is currently being developed into an online program series and possibly more. To that end I spend most of my time writing and developing the series at present so just don't have the time.

Question: Do I Need to Have A Drum Teacher as Well?

TSD ANSWER: Although the series is universal and can be studied alone, we believe all students of drums should at some time take private lessons from a local tutor or more than one tutor at various times within their development.

This is because every tutor teaches something different and may have a solution you may need to work on for your personal advancement.

Question: Are There Updates Available?

TSD ANSWER: Updates may become available for the PDF version booklets and so every customer will be automatically informed of updated versions.

Question: What Do I Get If I Start on The Course?

TSD ANSWER: If you decide to take the whole course then each part includes:

> A booklet with step-by-step instruction and written exercises. PDF format. (Not printable)
>
> An Audio of all exercise's demonstrated for you. MP3 Format.
>
> Paperback versions are also available as additions.

Or, you may receive both of the above-mentioned versions depending on your personal choice.

Question: Why Doesn't the Course Include Videos?

TSD ANSWER: Again, if you practice 10 hours per day and achieve a high level of success, do you think you would achieve that same success by spending half that time watching someone else play? No - you do not need to see how to do something you need to HEAR how to do something. Then move onto something else/the next thing.

Sitting watching videos is great for analyzing how someone else does things –
Actively listening and seeing something written leaves no margin for personal judgment as a video does.

To repeat, videos are great for analyzing someone else - your job as the student is to analyze yourself. In short, videos are a secondary process and mainly for more advanced players.

Through the program, you will receive recommendations for which videos outside of the course you will require in order to help make you the great drummer.

Question: Can the Program Really Make Me a Great Drummer?

TSD ANSWER: As already touched upon in the last questions it is "what you do within the time that you have" that can make you a great drummer. Only you can decide your level of success. Completing the program will not make you a great drummer. Perfecting and mastering each of these course parts will.

Question: Can You Explain the Time Space & Drums Formula Some More?

TSD ANSWER: The most valuable commodity in the universe is TIME. What you do "WITH your time" determines your level of achievement in any subject area. What you do "IN your time" (what you fill the space with) determines your level of mastery within that subject area.

For example, you may practice 10 hours per day and achieve a modicum of success. Practice the same amount of time per day doing THE RIGHT things WITHIN those 10 hours makes the greatest difference. The real secret is having a planned-out route which is what the Time Space & Drums Series is.

Question: Why Do You Speak of The Universe?

TSD ANSWER: The universe concept is a metaphor only. The creation of the universe itself began with the big bang, then stars were formed, constellations of stars, galaxies, etc. The universe serves as a valuable metaphor to create and develop your skills.

As an example, part one of the course is titled "Gravity" - Getting Grounded (Rock Style). The universe serves as a valuable metaphor to create and develop your skills starting with gravity - getting grounded - building a foundation.

Faster and increased understanding comes from knowing and understanding the smallest atomic units or parts of any subject area, which again is what The Time Space & drums Series covers.

Question: I Don't Have A Great Deal of Time to Practice. Will That Be A Problem?

TSD ANSWER: One of the great advantages of a home study program is that you can work at your own pace. You can schedule your practice, daily, weekly, or monthly if you so wish. The course packages can be downloaded each time you order a course part. So, you can order Part 2 as soon as you have completed part 1. Or you can wait a week or two whilst you perfect part one completely and so on.

Question: What If There Is Something I Don't Understand on The Course?

TSD ANSWER: If you have any questions or other queries about any aspect of the course, they will be answered, in writing, by myself or my colleagues, (Other Experienced Drummers). Just register and use the Answers section at timespaceanddrums.com

Question: Do I Have to Take the Whole Course?

TSD ANSWER: Of course, the intention is to complete all of the series parts, but you can withdraw from the program at any time if you order individual series parts to download. *(If you decide then to order the whole course you can do so and receive a discount based on the parts you've ordered so far.)* There is no penalty for this whatsoever and no obligation beyond the lesson files already received.

Question: What Do I Need to Get Started on The Program?

TSD ANSWER: You can start learning from the program providing you have: A metronome, a wooden practice kit, a bass drum pedal, and a hi-hat pedal. You can then purchase a full drum kit if you wish. As and when you need it.

Question: How Do I Start on The Program?

TSD ANSWER: Answer: You can order part one now by searching Amazon for Rock Drumming Foundation Course. Add part one to your shopping cart and follow the usual Amazon checkout process.

Question: What Makes This Course So Different?

TSD ANSWER: Generally drumming books can be divided into two categories. The beginner and the advanced player. The books written with the beginner in mind teach basic rhythms and or rudimentary exercises. One would have to read music and have a good level of experience and independence to play the first exercises in these books. The lack of usable rhythms is very apparent in these books.

The titles aimed at the advanced player are mostly Great American Drummers teaching the very advanced artistic approaches to play the drums. The rhythms are very complicated in most cases and the majority of them rely on the student having a lot of experience and practice behind him or her with a solid foundation already in place.

The Time Space & Drum Series takes you right to the very beginning and Step by Step, exercise by exercise, the student develops a foundation, then begins to build on that foundation to create an even better foundation.

The Time Space & Drum Series contains all of what several books, videos, and tapes on the market today will teach you. And much more. The Time & Space Course Files puts all of the knowledge and exercises in the order they should be learned, studied, and mastered.

To illustrate, of what use is having the knowledge to play complicated rhythms and fills, if the student can't keep time, or a basic rhythm going for any length of time without speeding up or slowing down. The basic drumming skills are essential for success.

CONCLUSION

Well, that about covers The Time Space & Drum Common Drumming Questions. All is left for me to do is to hope that you attained some values for even one of the questions or many questions.

I have been informed that reading the answers to many of the questions helps drummers to carve a drumming path that removes even more obstacles and allows them to embark on a much smoother hassle-free journey.

Again, thank you for your support.

Stephen Hawkins

Time Space & Drums.

Closing Note:

The Time Space and Drums series is intended as a complete program from Part 1 to Part 12, plus supplemental books. It is strongly advised that you follow the program in order of the parts as they integrate and build on each other.

Mastery comes from paying attention to the most basic fundamentals already covered in each of the exercises within this book series.

Ask the Author and Other Drummers

Although we have endeavored to answer all of the most common questions asked by the drummer just starting out. You may have a specific question that you want an answer to that isn't covered here. To that end, we added a Yahoo Answers-style Questioning System at the Time Space and Drums Community. To use the system to ask the author and other drummers anything simply register at the new TimeSpaceAndDrums drumming community here - timespaceanddrums.com

After registering go to your Profile User Control Panel and click the Answers Button in the main button section.

What's Next

Thank you for choosing Time Space and Drums as one of your learning tools. I hope you enjoyed the process. You can explore more of the series in Gravity Volume One and Two, the first and second books in the series by searching for either **Rock Drumming Foundation"** or "**Jazz Drumming Foundation**" at your favorite bookstore.

Share Your Experience

If you have a moment, please review this Common Drumming Questions book at the store where you bought it. Help other drummers and tell them why you enjoyed the book or what could be improved. Thank you!

Thank you again dear reader and I hope we meet again between the pages of another book. Remember, You rock!

Other Books by The Author

Modern Drumming Concepts
Rock Drumming Foundation Series part. (Six in-depth Drum Lessons).
Jazz Drumming Foundation Series part. (Six in-depth Drum Lessons).
Rock Drumming Development Series part. (Six in-depth Drum Lessons).
Jazz Drumming Development Series part. (Six in-depth Drum Lessons).
Odd Time Drumming Foundation Series part. (Six in-depth Drum Lessons).
Music Minus Drummer Collection. (Six in-depth Drum Lessons).
Accents and Phrasing Series part. (Four in-depth Drum Lessons).
Basic Latin Drumming Foundation Series part. (Four in-depth Drum Lessons).
Developing Creativity Volume 1. (Four in-depth Drum Lessons).
Developing Creativity Volume 2. (Four in-depth Drum Lessons).
Developing Creativity Volume 3. (Five in-depth Drum Lessons).
Developing Creativity Volume 4. (Six in-depth Drum Lessons).

www.ingramcontent.com/pod-product-compliance
Lightning Source LLC
Chambersburg PA
CBHW081356080526
44588CB00016B/2512